first book of
aircraft

Isabel Thomas

For Harry, Joey and Oscar

Published 2013 by
A&C Black
An imprint of Bloomsbury Publishing Plc
50 Bedford Square, London, WC1B 3DP

www.bloomsbury.com

ISBN 978-1-4081-9293-1

A CIP catalogue for this book is available from the British Library.

This book is produced using paper that is made from wood
grown in managed, sustainable forests. It is natural, renewable
and recyclable. The logging and manufacturing processes
conform to the environmental regulations of the country of origin.

Printed in China by C&C.

10 9 8 7 6 5 4 3 2 1

MIX
Paper from
responsible sources
FSC® C008047
www.fsc.org

Contents

Introduction   5

Hot air balloon   6
Airship   7
Hang glider   8
Paraglider   9
Helicopter   10–11
Gyroplane   12
Light aircraft   13
Microlight   14
Glider   15
Stunt plane   16
Business aircraft   17
Cargo plane   18–19
Twin prop aeroplane   20
Twin jet aeroplane   21
Trijet aeroplane   22
Jumbo jet   23
Superjumbo   24–25
Supersonic jet   26
Vintage aircraft   27

Biplane   28

Triplane   29

Combat aircraft   30

Strike aircraft   31

Tiltrotor   32–33

Unmanned Aircraft System (UAS) 34

Flying wing   35

Vertical take-off and landing jet   36

Flying car   37

Seaplane   38–39

Space plane   40

Useful words   41

Spotter's guide   42-47

Find out more   48

Aircraft safety
Aircraft are powerful machines. They can be very dangerous.
Always have an adult with you when you look at aircraft.
Do not stand close to aircraft.

Aircraft

The sky is full of exciting flying machines.
Look out for gliders and hot air balloons.
Listen out for the roar of a jet plane and
the buzz of helicopters.

You can spot aircraft at airports, air shows,
museums, and in the sky. This book will
help you to name the aircraft you see. It
tells you how they work and shows you
what special features to look out for.

At the back of this book is a Spotter's
Guide to help you remember the aircraft
you find. Tick them off as you spot them.
You can also find out the meaning of
some useful words here.

Turn the page to find out all about aircraft!

Hot air balloon

Look for colourful hot air balloons on sunny days. They carry passengers over countryside and cities. The pilot can make the balloon go up or down. It travels slowly, in the same direction as the wind.

Balloon made of nylon

The burner heats the air inside the balloon. The hot air rises.

The pilot lands by letting hot air out of the balloon. The balloon sinks back to the ground.

Skirt made of fireproof material

Burner

Wicker basket carries passengers

Fuel tanks

Airship

An airship is like a huge helium balloon. It is filled with a gas that is lighter than air. The gas helps the airship to rise up into the air without using much engine power.

This airship carries tourists in California, USA.

Layers of fabric and plastic

Plastic and metal frame inside

Longer than a jumbo jet

Rear engine pushes the airship through the air

Two pilots

Cabin for up to 12 passengers

Side engine steers the airship

Fins help with steering

Hang glider

Hang glider pilots swoop and soar like birds, hanging below a giant wing. Hang gliders do not have engines. They hitch a lift on rising warm air.

The wing is made of fabric wrapped around a metal skeleton.

Helmet

Triangle-shaped wing

Hang glider pilots launch themselves off hillsides, or get towed into the air.

Wires

Harness

Control bar

The pilot steers by moving her body from side to side.

Paraglider

This parachute does not drop from a plane. It takes off from the ground! The pilot sits in a special harness. She steers the paraglider by moving her body, and pulling cables.

Paragliders are the only aircraft that can be packed into a rucksack.

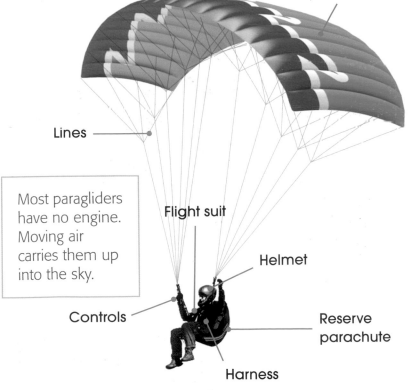

Soft fabric sail

Lines

Most paragliders have no engine. Moving air carries them up into the sky.

Flight suit

Helmet

Controls

Reserve parachute

Harness

Helicopter

Rotors let helicopters fly forwards, backwards, and sideways. They don't need a runway to take off and land. Helicopters can also hover. This lets them pick things up without landing.

Tail rotor for steering

Helicopters are very useful in an emergency. This rescue helicopter picks up injured people in the mountains.

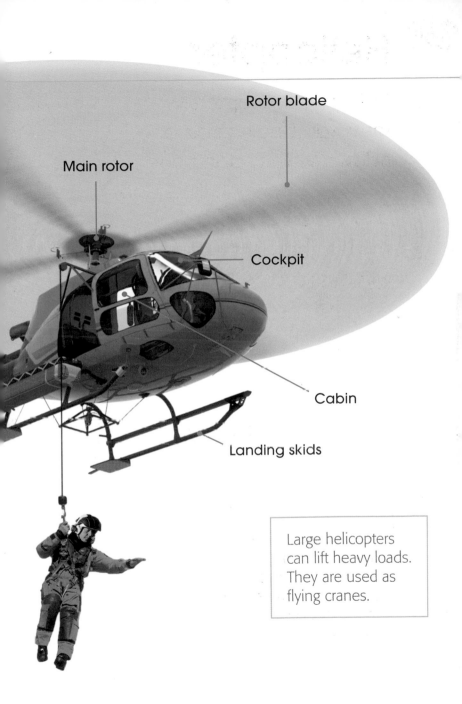

Rotor blade

Main rotor

Cockpit

Cabin

Landing skids

Large helicopters can lift heavy loads. They are used as flying cranes.

Gyroplane

This aircraft looks like a helicopter. But it works in a different way. A propeller engine pushes the gyroplane forwards. The rotor blades are pushed around by air, like a windmill. This lifts the gyroplane into the air.

Rotor blades tilted backwards

Propeller

No tail rotor

A gyroplane cannot hover.

Engine

Light aircraft

Light aircraft are the cars of the sky. People learn to fly them for fun, and for sport. They are also used as small business, passenger, and cargo planes.

This Cessna Caravan carries up to 14 passengers.

Wings high on body

Wheels do not fold into fuselage

Piston engine

Propeller

Microlight

These tiny aircraft are like hang gliders with engines. Wheels let them take off and land on flat ground. You might spot one taking off from a beach.

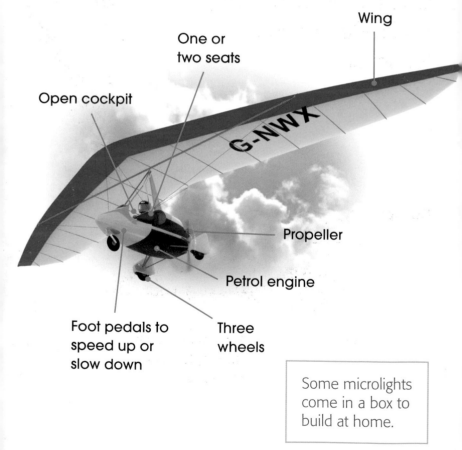

Wing

One or two seats

Open cockpit

G-NWX

Propeller

Petrol engine

Foot pedals to speed up or slow down

Three wheels

Some microlights come in a box to build at home.

Glider

You might spot gliders in the countryside. Most gliders do not have an engine. They are towed or launched into the air. Once they are up, they can glide and soar for hours.

People fly gliders for fun and for sport.

Winglet

Very long, thin wing

Cockpit

Fuselage made from light, strong material

G-NNAB

Stunt plane

This plane is specially designed for stunts. It is light but very strong. Look out for planes like this at air shows. They roll, spin, and loop-the-loop to amaze the crowds.

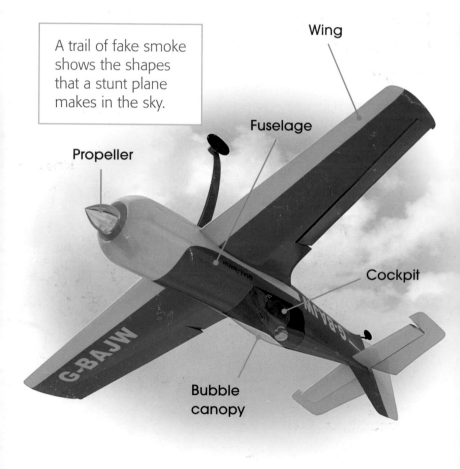

A trail of fake smoke shows the shapes that a stunt plane makes in the sky.

Wing

Fuselage

Propeller

Cockpit

G-BAJW

Bubble canopy

Business aircraft

A private plane is useful for people who fly often for work. It can travel wherever they need to go, whenever they want to leave. The fastest business aircraft have jet engines.

The cabin of this Learjet is a comfortable place to work. Passengers can even hold meetings in the air.

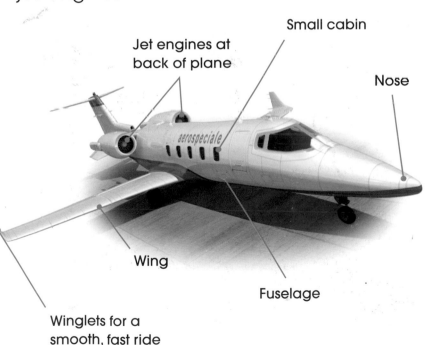

Jet engines at back of plane

Small cabin

Nose

Wing

Fuselage

Winglets for a smooth, fast ride

Cargo plane

These huge aircraft carry goods
from place to place. There is a
large door at the back or front.
Sometimes the whole nose lifts up to
load and unload cargo.

Nose visor (front-
loading door)

Cargo

FastT

Cargo planes carry things that
need to be delivered quickly,
such as post and fresh food.

Some cargo planes can drop their load while they are flying. The goods are attached to parachutes and fall slowly to the ground.

No passenger windows

Passenger planes also carry cargo.

Landing gear with lots of wheels

The biggest cargo planes have humped bodies. They can carry extra-large cargo, such as other aircraft.

Twin prop aeroplane

This airliner has two turboprop engines. These are jet engines that turn propellers. You can spot them on airliners that make short or medium-sized journeys.

Many cargo planes have turboprop engines.

Six-blade propeller

Narrow fuselage with one aisle

Turboprop engine

Turboprop engines can be very noisy.

Twin jet aeroplane

Most airliners have turbofan jet engines. These engines are smooth, quiet and fast. Small and medium-sized airliners only need two jet engines.

Boeing 737s carry millions of people on holiday every year.

Tail decorated with airline logo

Main deck for passengers and crew

6 passengers in each row of seats

Birdproof windshield

Cargo deck for luggage and cargo

Trijet aeroplane

Aeroplanes powered by three jet engines are tricky to spot. Very few are made each year. Their extra engine makes them very safe to fly. If one engine breaks down, the plane still has two engines to land with.

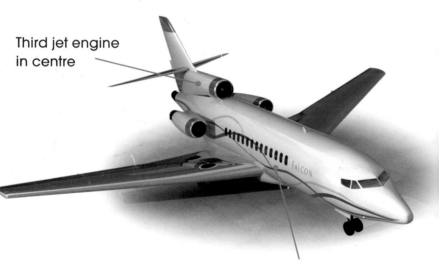

Third jet engine in centre

FALCON

Cabin with room for 19 passengers

This Dassault Falcon is being used as a business jet.

Jumbo jet

The biggest jet airliners are known as jumbo jets. They usually fly long distances. They can fit up to ten passengers in every row.

Forty-five cars could fit on the wing of this Boeing 747.

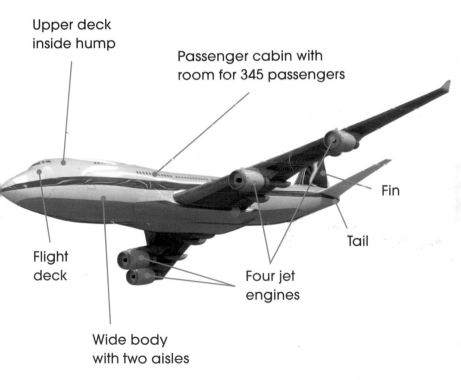

Upper deck inside hump

Passenger cabin with room for 345 passengers

Fin

Tail

Flight deck

Four jet engines

Wide body with two aisles

Superjumbo

If you visit an airport,
look out for an
Airbus A380.

**Full-length
upper deck**

The A380 is so
big, there are
lifts between
its decks.

AIRBUS A380

It is the world's biggest airliner. More than 800 passengers can fly at once.

Lower deck

First class passengers can book private rooms with full-sized beds.

Four jet engines

Supersonic jet

Supersonic aircraft can fly faster than sound travels. Look out for supersonic military planes. If one flies past, you will hear a loud boom, like thunder.

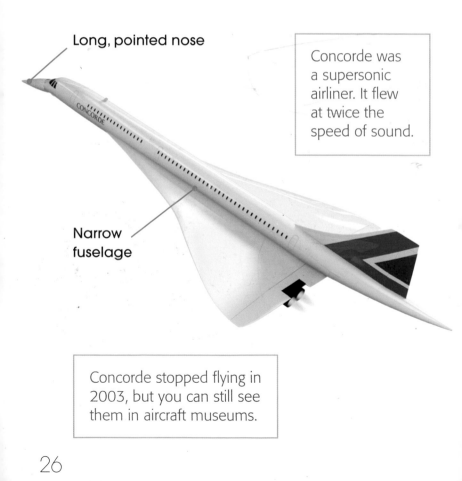

Long, pointed nose

Narrow fuselage

Concorde was a supersonic airliner. It flew at twice the speed of sound.

Concorde stopped flying in 2003, but you can still see them in aircraft museums.

Vintage aircraft

At aircraft museums, you can climb onboard aircraft from the past. But it's even better to see one fly! Many old aircraft have been kept working. You can see them in action at air shows.

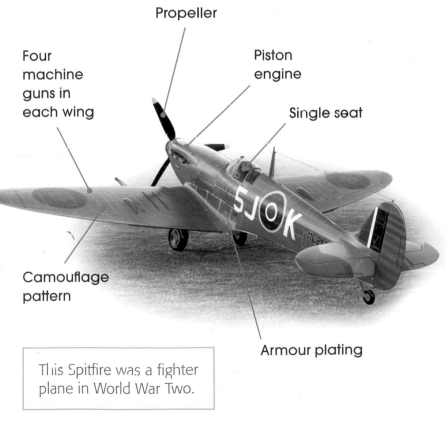

Propeller

Four machine guns in each wing

Piston engine

Single seat

Camouflage pattern

Armour plating

This Spitfire was a fighter plane in World War Two.

Biplane

Biplanes have two wings on each side. The wings are joined together by struts.

The world's first proper aeroplane was a biplane, called the Wright Flyer.

Upper wing

Strut

Lower wing

The extra wings let this biplane fly very slowly. This is useful for spraying crops, or putting out forest fires.

Triplane

Some of the very first aeroplanes had three wings on each side. They are called triplanes. This one was a fighter plane in World War One.

Triplanes are slower than other types of planes. They are very rare today.

Strut

Open cockpit

Wooden propeller

Combat aircraft

This fighter jet is one of the most amazing aircraft in the world. It can fly faster than the speed of sound. Powerful computers help it to find and attack enemy targets in the sky.

Sleek fuselage for supersonic speed

Weapons stored inside fuselage

Ejection seat

Special shape helps it hide from enemy radar

Ejection seats blast fighter pilots out of their plane in an emergency.

Strike aircraft

Bombers attack enemy targets on the ground. They are specially designed to carry heavy loads.

Tail fin

Wings swing back for high speed flight

Seat for a weapons operator

Pilot

Weapons carried under fuselage and wings

When this Tornado takes off, its wings stick straight out to the side. This helps lift the plane into the sky. The wings swing back for flying at high speed.

Tiltrotor

What do you get if you cross an aeroplane with a helicopter? A tiltrotor! This amazing aircraft can tilt its engines as it flies.

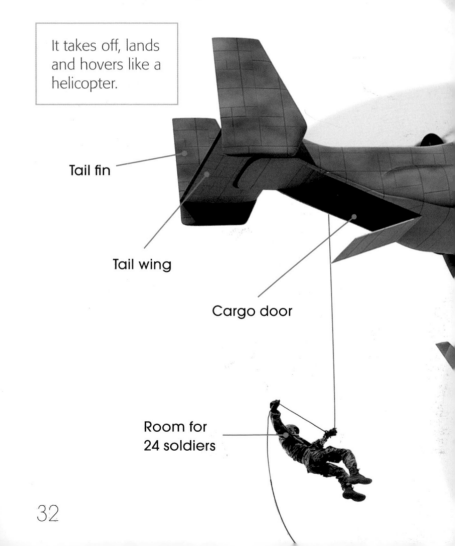

It takes off, lands and hovers like a helicopter.

Tail fin

Tail wing

Cargo door

Room for 24 soldiers

Large propeller

But it can also
zoom through
the sky as
quickly as an
aeroplane.

Wing

Turboprop
engine

Unmanned Aircraft System (UAS)

What is missing from this aeroplane?
The pilot! A powerful computer
flies the plane.

Unmanned military aircraft
can fly into dangerous
areas. No pilot is in danger
if they are attacked.

Antenna for sending
signals back to base

Propeller

engine

No cockpit

Small, light
fuselage

Unmanned aircraft have been
flown into hurricanes and cyclones.
They send information back to
scientists on the ground.

Flying wing

Flying wings have no fuselage or tail. The cockpit, engines, fuel tanks and cargo are all inside one large, triangle-shaped wing.

Flying wings travel very smoothly through the air. This helps military aircraft to hide from enemies.

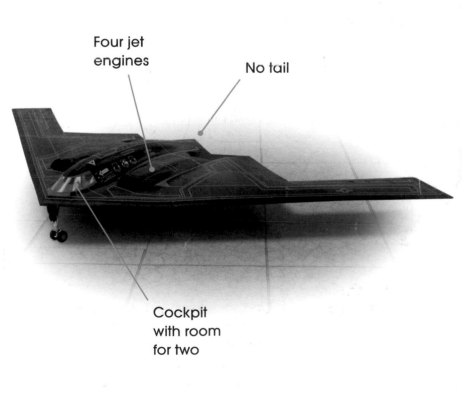

Four jet engines

No tail

Cockpit with room for two

Vertical take-off and landing jet

This is a special plane. Its jet engine has a nozzle that can be pointed downwards. This lets it hover in the air, and land without a runway.

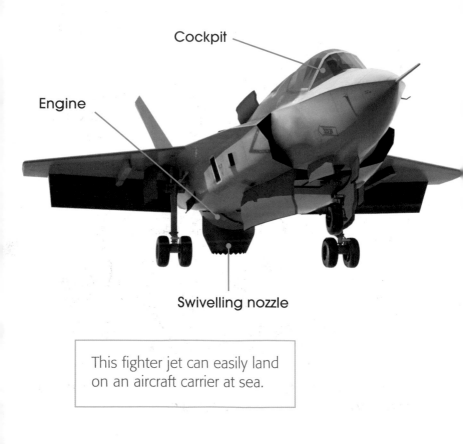

Cockpit

Engine

Swivelling nozzle

This fighter jet can easily land on an aircraft carrier at sea.

Flying car

Folding the wings of this aeroplane turns it into a road vehicle. It can be kept in a normal garage. The pilot can drive it to the airport!

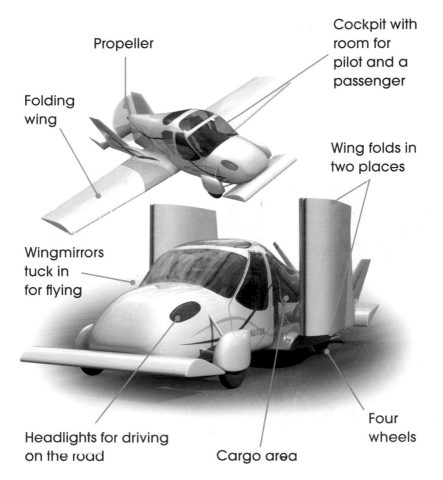

Propeller

Cockpit with room for pilot and a passenger

Folding wing

Wing folds in two places

Wingmirrors tuck in for flying

Headlights for driving on the road

Cargo area

Four wheels

Seaplane

Seaplanes can take off and land on water. They can fly to places where there are no airports, such as small islands.

An amphibious plane can take off and land from runways, as well as water.

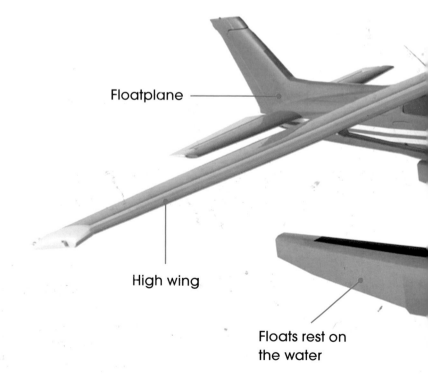

Fuselage rests on water

Floatplane

High wing

Floats rest on the water

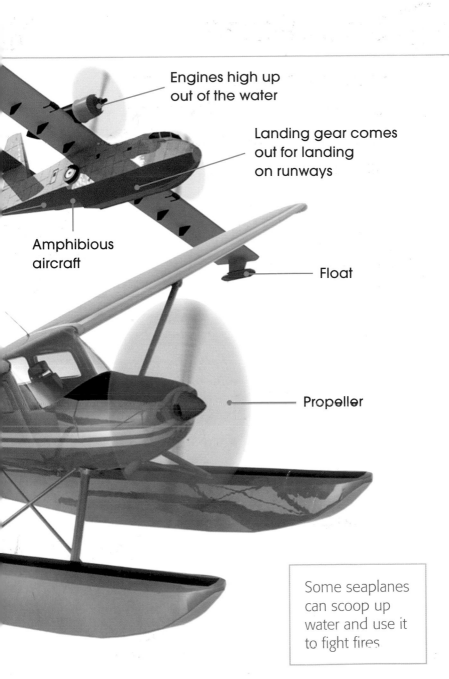

Engines high up
out of the water

Landing gear comes
out for landing
on runways

Amphibious
aircraft

Float

Propeller

Some seaplanes
can scoop up
water and use it
to fight fires

Space plane

A powerful rocket engine blasts this aircraft into space. It uses its wings to glide back down to Earth afterwards.

Wings don't work in space because there is no air. A space plane flies like a spaceship in space, using thrusters to steer.

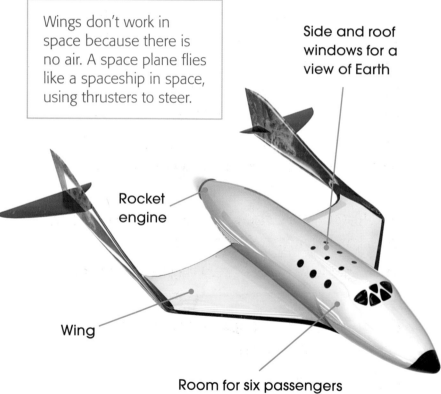

Side and roof windows for a view of Earth

Rocket engine

Wing

Room for six passengers and two pilots

Useful words

cabin the place where passengers sit

cockpit where the pilot sits

flight deck where the pilot and crew sit
on a large aircraft

fuselage the body of an aeroplane

jet engine an engine that burns fuel to
produce a jet of hot gas and move an
aircraft forwards

landing gear the wheels that an aircraft
rests on when it's not flying

piston engine an engine that burns fuel
to move pistons up and down, which
turns a propeller

propeller blades that spin around vertically,
pushing an aircraft forwards

rotor blades that spin around horizontally,
lifting an aircraft into the air

wing the part that supports the rest
of the aircraft in the air

winglet the turned-up end of some
aeroplane wings, to help the plane
to travel more smoothly through the air

Spotter's guide

How many of these aircraft have you seen? Tick them when you spot them.

Hot air balloon
page 6

Airship
page 7

Hang glider
page 8

Paraglider
page 9

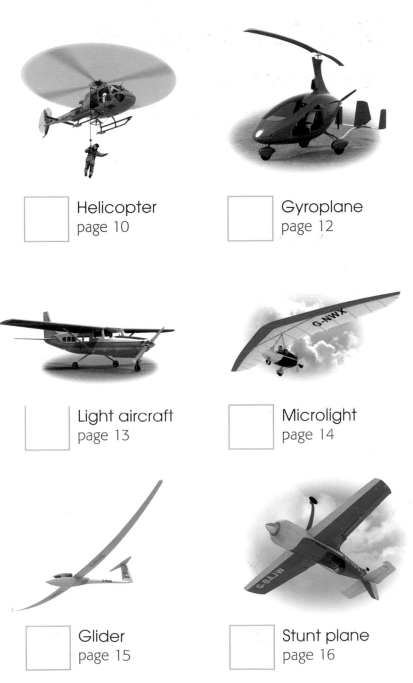

Helicopter
page 10

Gyroplane
page 12

Light aircraft
page 13

Microlight
page 14

Glider
page 15

Stunt plane
page 16

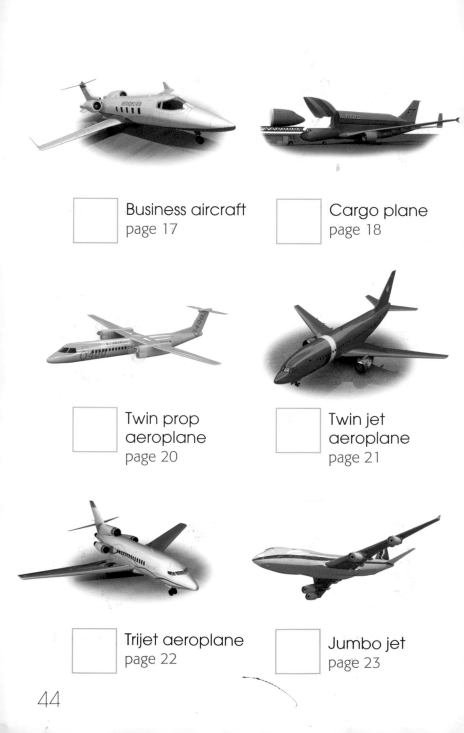

Business aircraft
page 17

Cargo plane
page 18

Twin prop
aeroplane
page 20

Twin jet
aeroplane
page 21

Trijet aeroplane
page 22

Jumbo jet
page 23

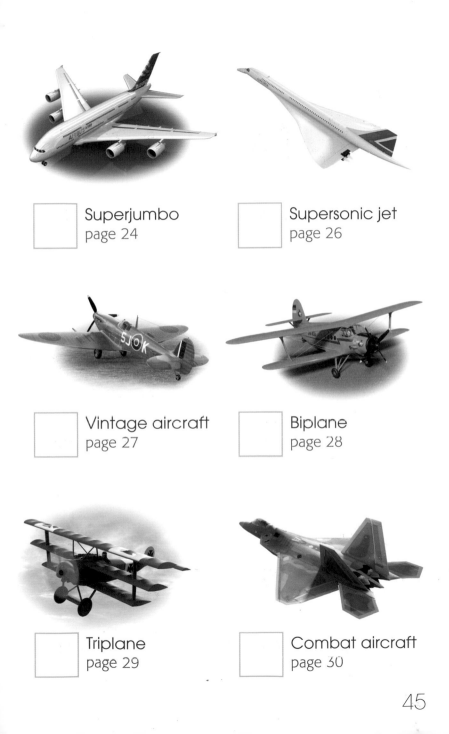

Superjumbo
page 24

Supersonic jet
page 26

Vintage aircraft
page 27

Biplane
page 28

Triplane
page 29

Combat aircraft
page 30

45

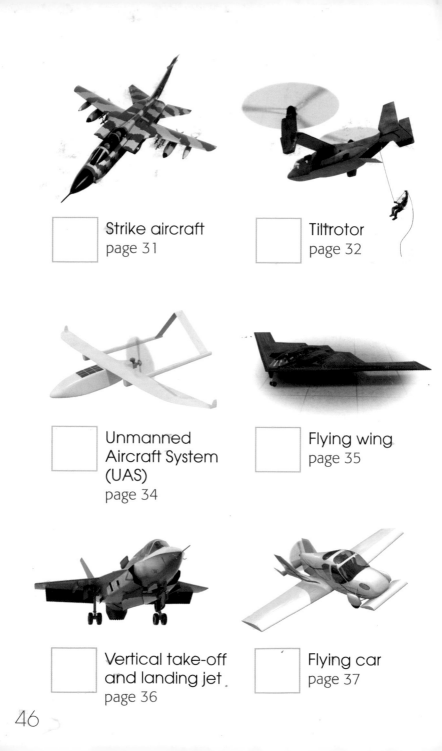

☐ Strike aircraft
page 31

☐ Tiltrotor
page 32

☐ Unmanned Aircraft System (UAS)
page 34

☐ Flying wing
page 35

☐ Vertical take-off and landing jet
page 36

☐ Flying car
page 37

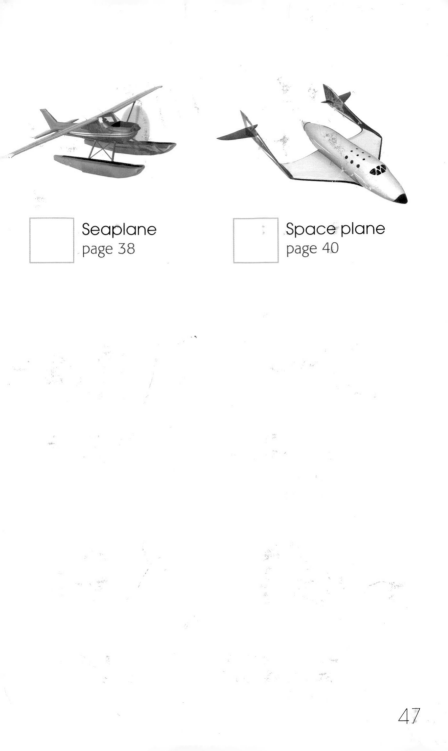

Seaplane
page 38

Space plane
page 40

Find out more

If you would like to find out more about aircraft, you could visit an aircraft museum or air show. You can also look at these websites.

Imperial War Museum Duxford
www.iwm.org.uk/visits/iwm-duxford

Yorkshire Air Museum
www.yorkshireairmuseum.org/

Royal Airforce Museum London and Cosford
www.rafmuseum.org.uk

Royal International Air Tattoo
www.airtattoo.com/

Farnborough International Airshow
www.farnborough.com/